BOOK SOL
NO LONGER THE
PROPERTIC

PUBLIC LIBRARY
AUG 19 2015
CENTRAL LIBRARY
905-884-9288

D0096463

Collins English R

Amazing Women

Level 1
CEF A2

Text by
Helen Parker

Series edited by
Fiona MacKenzie

rh

Collins

HarperCollins Publishers
77–85 Fulham Palace Road
Hammersmith, London W6 8JB

10 9 8 7 6 5 4 3 2 1

Original text
© The Amazing People Club Ltd

Adapted text
© HarperCollins Publishers 2013

ISBN: 978-0-00-754493-6

Collins® is a registered trademark of
HarperCollins Publishers Limited

www.collinselt.com

A catalogue record for this book is available
from the British Library

Printed in the UK by Martins the Printers

All rights reserved. No part of this book
may be reproduced, stored in a retrieval
system, or transmitted in any form or
by any means, electronic, mechanical,
photocopying, recording or otherwise,
without the prior permission in writing
of the Publisher. This book is sold subject
to the conditions that it shall not, by way
of trade or otherwise, be lent, re-sold,
hired out or otherwise circulated without
the Publisher's prior consent in any form
of binding or cover other than that in
which it is published and without a similar
condition including this condition being
imposed on the subsequent purchaser.

HarperCollins does not warrant that
www.collinselt.com or any other website
mentioned in this title will be provided
uninterrupted, that any website will be
error free, that defects will be corrected, or
that the website or the server that makes it
available are free of viruses or bugs. For full
terms and conditions please refer to the site
terms provided on the website.

These readers are based on original texts
(BioViews®) published by The Amazing
People Club group.® BioViews® and The
Amazing People Club® are registered
trademarks and represent the views of the
author.

BioViews® are scripted virtual interview
based on research about a person's life and
times. As in any story, the words are only
an interpretation of what the individuals
mentioned in the BioViews® could have
said. Although the interpretations are
based on available research, they do not
purport to represent the actual views of
the people mentioned. The interpretations
are made in good faith, recognizing that
other interpretations could also be made.
The author and publisher disclaim any
responsibility from any action that readers
take regarding the BioViews® for educational
or other purposes. Any use of the BioViews®
materials is the sole responsibility of the
reader and should be supported by their own
independent research.

Cover image © sniegirova mariia/
Shutterstock

MIX
Paper from
responsible sources

FSC
www.fsc.org   FSC® C007454

FSC™ is a non-profit international organisation established to promote the
responsible management of the world's forests. Products carrying the FSC
label are independently certified to assure consumers that they come from
forests that are managed to meet the social, economic and ecological needs
of present and future generations, and other controlled sources.

Find out more about HarperCollins and the environment at
www.harpercollins.co.uk/green

◆ Contents ◆

✦ INTRODUCTION ✦

Collins Amazing People Readers are collections of short stories. Each book presents the life story of five or six people whose lives and achievements have made a difference to our world today. The stories are carefully graded to ensure that you, the reader, will both enjoy and benefit from your reading experience.

You can choose to enjoy the book from start to finish or to dip into your favourite story straight away. Each story is entirely independent.

After every story a short timeline brings together the most important events in each person's life into one short report. The timeline is a useful tool for revision purposes.

Words which are above the required reading level are underlined the first time they appear in each story. All underlined words are defined in the glossary at the back of the book. Levels 1 and 2 take their definitions from the *Collins COBUILD Essential English Dictionary* and levels 3 and 4 from the *Collins COBUILD Advanced English Dictionary*.

To support both teachers and learners, additional materials are available online at www.collinselt.com/readers.

The Amazing People Club®

Collins Amazing People Readers are adaptations of original texts published by The Amazing People Club. The Amazing People Club is an educational publishing house. It was founded in 2006 by educational psychologist and management leader Dr Charles Margerison and publishes books, eBooks, audio books, iBooks and video content, which bring readers 'face to face' with many of the world's most inspiring and influential characters from the fields of art, science, music, politics, medicine and business.

◆ THE GRADING SCHEME ◆

The Collins COBUILD Grading Scheme has been created using the most up-to-date language usage information available today. Each level is guided by a brand new comprehensive grammar and vocabulary framework, ensuring that the series will perfectly match readers' abilities.

		CEF band	Pages	Word count	Headwords
Level 1	elementary	A2	64	5,000–8,000	approx. 700
Level 2	pre-intermediate	A2–B1	80	8,000–11,000	approx. 900
Level 3	intermediate	B1	96	11,000–15,000	approx. 1,100
Level 4	upper intermediate	B2	112	15,000–19,000	approx. 1,700

For more information on the Collins COBUILD Grading Scheme, including a full list of the grammar structures found at each level, go to www.collinselt.com/readers/gradingscheme.

Also available online: Make sure that you are reading at the right level by checking your level on our website (www.collinselt.com/readers/levelcheck).

Harriet Tubman

◆ ◆ ◆

*c.*1820–1913

the slave who escaped and helped hundreds
of other slaves to escape

I escaped from <u>slavery</u> in the south of the USA. I then helped hundreds of other slaves to escape to the north of the USA and Canada. I also <u>freed</u> hundreds of slaves who wanted to fight in the <u>Civil War</u>.

◆ ◆ ◆

My parents were slaves for the Brodess family in Maryland, USA. I was the fifth of nine children. At the age of 6, I started work as a <u>nursemaid</u> for another family. After that I had to work in the woods and fields. Our <u>owners</u> did not think of us as people. For them, we were like animals or machines. If we did something wrong, they hit us or <u>punished</u> us in horrible ways.

In 1831, at the age of 11, I started to do the same work as the adult slaves. Every day we had to work for many hours in the fields. Around this time, I received an <u>injury</u>, which I never forgot. I refused to stop a slave who was escaping. The slave's owner threw a metal weight at the slave, but it hit me on the head. It hurt a lot and this injury gave me headaches for the rest of my life.

◆ ◆ ◆

In 1849, I was brave and tried to escape. I was married by then, but my <u>marriage</u> was very unhappy and I hated the thought of another year of slavery. Two of my brothers agreed to come with me. We wanted to reach the north of the USA, where slavery was <u>illegal</u>. I could live there as a <u>free</u> woman.

We <u>made</u> good <u>progress</u> towards the north, but then we heard some bad news. Our owner was offering $300 to anyone who caught us. My brothers became frightened and we decided to return to Maryland. We were punished when we returned, but I still wanted to escape.

A short time later, I escaped again. This time I went alone. I travelled at night along quiet roads and paths. Some kind people helped me on the way. They gave me food and a place to sleep. Finally, I arrived in the city of Philadelphia in the north. The journey was long and difficult, but it felt wonderful to be free at last.

◆ ◆ ◆

In Philadelphia, I got a job and began to earn money. I missed my parents and my brothers and sisters. I was free and I wanted my family to be free, too. Maybe I could help them to escape?

In 1850, I received some bad news. My niece and her daughters were in danger. Their owner wanted to sell them and they didn't want to go to different families. I decided to return to Maryland to free them. I had to help them to escape. We travelled at night and used the stars to <u>find our way</u> to the north.

After helping my niece and her daughters, I helped many other slaves to escape. I offered to help my husband, John Tubman, too, but he didn't want to leave the south. He didn't want to be with me any more, so our marriage ended.

Soon, a new <u>law</u> made things a lot more difficult for me. It became illegal to help a slave to escape in the USA. I had to find a new <u>route</u> – to Canada, where slavery was illegal.

◆ ◆ ◆

In 1857, I went on a very special journey to help my parents. They weren't slaves any more, but their life in the south was very difficult. They were very happy to see me again and wanted to go with me to Canada. Our journey was very slow and difficult because my parents were old. We had a big celebration when we finally arrived in Ontario, Canada.

In 1861, the American Civil War started. The Confederates from the south wanted slavery to continue. The Unionists from the north wanted slavery to become illegal. I joined the Union Army, which <u>fought for</u> the north. An army captain, James Montgomery, heard about me. He discovered that I helped slaves to escape before the war. And he wanted my help. He wanted slaves to fight for <u>freedom</u> in the Union Army. I took a team of <u>spies</u> to the south and found slaves who wanted to join us. It was dangerous work, but we were very <u>successful</u>. On one trip, 700 slaves agreed to escape and they became soldiers.

On 9th April 1865, the war ended. What could I do with my life now? I decided to fight for <u>equal</u> <u>rights</u> for black people and for women. I spoke at public meetings and I tried to help black people who were poor and old.

◆ ◆ ◆

In 1896, I bought some land and, in 1903, I gave the land to my church. I wanted the church to start a home for black people who were poor and elderly. In 1908, the home opened for the first time.

As I looked back at my life, I was very proud. I was happy that I helped so many people to find freedom.

The Life of Harriet Tubman

*c.*1820 Araminta Harriet Ross was born in Maryland, USA. Her parents were slaves for the Brodess family.

1826 She started to work as a nursemaid when she was 6 years old.

1831 When she was 11 years old, she started to do the same work as adult slaves. She was hit by a metal weight. The head injury gave her pain for the rest of her life.

1844 She married John Tubman, a free man.

1849 She escaped for the first time with two of her brothers. $300 was offered to anyone who caught them. They decided to return to their owner. A short time later, Harriet escaped again and reached Philadelphia in the north of the USA.

1850 She helped her niece and many other slaves to escape to Philadelphia. It became illegal to help a slave to escape in the USA. Harriet found a new route to Canada.

1857 She helped her parents to escape to Ontario, Canada.

1860   She went on her last journey to help slaves to escape from the south.

1861   Harriet joined the Union Army in the Civil War.

1863   She worked for Colonel James Montgomery, a captain in the Union Army. She found slaves who wanted to join the Union Army.

1865   She wrote a book *Scenes in the Life of Harriet Tubman* with Sarah H. Bradford.

1869   She married Nelson Davis who was a soldier in the Civil War.

1899   She started to receive money for her work during the war.

1903   She bought some land to build a home for black people who were poor and old.

1908   The Harriet Tubman Home for the Aged opened for the first time.

1913   Harriet died when she was 93 years old. She spent her final years in the home that she helped to build.

Emmeline Pankhurst

◆ ◆ ◆

1858–1928

the woman who wanted women to be able to vote

I <u>campaigned</u> all my life for <u>equal</u> <u>rights</u> for women. I started a political group which <u>fought for</u> the <u>vote</u> for women in Britain. After many years of <u>protests</u>, we finally won the right for British women to <u>vote</u>.

◆ ◆ ◆

When I was born in 1858, women in Britain didn't have the same rights as men. Most women couldn't go to school or university. They were only allowed to work in certain jobs. And they didn't have the right to vote.

I grew up in Manchester in the north of England and I saw many problems every day. Mothers had to bring up children in small, dirty houses. <u>Disease</u> was everywhere because of the terrible conditions. And most women only lived until they were around 50 years old. I knew from a young age that I wanted to improve women's lives.

My parents believed in human rights. They believed that education was a right for women as well as men. In 1873, my parents sent me to school in Paris. They wanted me to get a wider view of the world.

◆ ◆ ◆

In Paris, I was disappointed to discover that women were still not equal with men after the French <u>Revolution</u>. <u>Action</u> was needed and I returned to England to begin the fight.

In Britain, the political situation was quite unusual. Our ruler was a woman, Queen Victoria. She was a <u>powerful</u> leader, but she wasn't interested in women's rights. Our politicians were all men and they definitely weren't interested in political <u>equality</u> for women.

In 1879, I was surprised to discover a man who was campaigning for women's rights. His name was Richard Pankhurst and he was a <u>lawyer</u>. We shared many of the same <u>beliefs</u> and ideas. We got married and started a family.

◆ ◆ ◆

For almost 20 years, Richard and I fought for political rights for women. Then, sadly, my dear husband died. My daughters and I were very sad, but we decided to continue our <u>campaign</u>. The two oldest daughters, Christabel and Sylvia, became <u>activists</u>. In 1903, we started the Women's Social and Political Union (WSPU). It was a group that fought for the right for women to

vote. Christabel became one of our bravest leaders. Sylvia was an artist and she designed our posters and signs.

The WSPU organized many public meetings and protests. Sometimes the police <u>arrested</u> our members. Christabel was one of the first to go to prison. When our members were in prison, we <u>protested</u>. And when our members came out of prison, we <u>celebrated</u> in the streets. It was very important to get public attention.

Unfortunately, the government didn't agree with our campaign. We had to take more powerful action. Some of our members began to break the <u>law</u>. They lit fires in buildings and broke windows. Our campaign was a war for these women. For me, it was always a fight for equal rights.

Every time I was arrested, I told the <u>judge</u>, 'We don't want to break laws, we want to make new laws.' But the lawyers and politicians didn't want to listen.

In 1910, Prime Minister Asquith, the government leader, stopped a new law that gave women the vote. We were shocked and angry. On Friday, 18th November, I led a group of women to meet the Prime Minister, but he refused to see us. We started to protest in the street and 100 women were arrested. It was a terrible day. We called it 'Black Friday'.

◆ ◆ ◆

In 1914 the First World War began and we agreed to stop our campaign. Women were now needed as nurses in hospitals and to work in factories and on farms. In 1917, we started a new group with a new name, The Women's Party. In 1918, the First World War ended. The government realized that women were an important part of the <u>victory</u> in the war.

At last, women were given the right to vote – but only women over 30 years old who owned a home could vote. Any man over 21 could vote. We still didn't have full equality!

After the war, I went to live in the USA, Canada and also Bermuda. In 1926, I returned to England. I wanted to become a politician, but my health wasn't good enough. In 1928, only three weeks before I died, a new law gave women the same right to vote as men. It took much longer than we hoped. But in the end our campaign was <u>successful</u> and at last we won political equality for women.

The Life of Emmeline Pankhurst

1858   Emmeline Goulden was born in Manchester, England.

1860s   She became interested in women's rights as a child and went to political meetings.

1873   She was sent to a school in Paris, which believed in equal education for boys and girls.

1879   She met and married Richard Pankhurst, a lawyer. He believed in votes for women.

1886   The family moved to London. They had meetings for political activists in their home.

1893   Richard and Emmeline returned to Manchester.

1898   Richard died, but Emmeline decided to continue the campaign to win the vote for women.

1903   Emmeline and her daughters, Christabel and Sylvia, started the Women's Social and Political Union (WSPU), which fought for political equality for women.

1905   Christabel was arrested during a protest.

1908   Emmeline was arrested for the first time. She went to prison for six weeks.

1910   Prime Minister Asquith stopped a law that gave women the vote. The WSPU protested and 100 women were arrested.

1914   The First World War started. The WSPU stopped their campaign for the vote.

1916   Emmeline visited the USA, Canada and Russia. She wanted women there to fight for the vote in their countries.

1917   Christabel and Emmeline started The Women's Party.

1918   The First World War ended. Women over 30 years old won the right to vote. After the war, Emmeline went to live in the USA, Canada and Bermuda.

1926   She returned to England and wanted to become a politician. She became ill and could not continue with her plans.

1928   Emmeline died in London a few weeks after a new law gave equal voting rights to women. She was 69 years old.

Maria Montessori

◆ ◆ ◆

1870–1952

the doctor who discovered a new
way to teach children

I was the first woman to get a <u>medical</u> degree in Italy. I helped children with <u>mental</u> problems to learn. I then <u>created</u> a special method to teach all children. Many schools around the world still use my method.

♦ ◆ ♦

When I was a little girl, my mother always told me, 'Be kind to others.' Every day, she asked me to make clothes for poor people. We lived in Chiaravalle in Italy and a lot of poor families lived near our home.

Fortunately, my parents had enough money to send me to school. My father had traditional ideas about women. He wanted me to get married and stay at home. So he didn't want me to continue my education after primary school. But my mother was very different and she encouraged me to study.

In 1883, I started at secondary school and after that I went to a <u>technical</u> college. I did well in maths and physics, but later I became very interested in biology. I decided to become a doctor. It wasn't an easy decision to make. Only men studied for medical degrees at that time. Would a medical school <u>accept</u> me?

◆ ◆ ◆

In 1890, I began a course in science at the University of Rome. I did very well in this degree and at last the university's medical school accepted me. Some of the teachers and students didn't want me to study there. But I worked hard and in 1896, I was the first woman in Italy to become a doctor.

The university had a special hospital for children with mental problems. I wanted to help the children to communicate and to learn. I wanted to improve their lives. But how could I do this? I began to study and give talks about this question.

In 1898, I became a director of a school in Rome for children with mental problems. At that time, people called these children horrible things, such as 'crazy' or 'idiots'. But these children were just different. And they needed to learn in a different way. My teachers and I *showed* the children what to do. Slowly, we <u>made progress</u> with this practical method. We showed the children simple <u>actions</u>, such as how to eat or wash or play games. The children copied these actions and then we repeated them again and again.

◆ ◆ ◆

In 1906, the government asked me to work in a different school for very young children from poor families. I changed the classrooms and took away the rows of desks. We used small tables and encouraged the children to play. We created <u>educational</u> toys that the children could touch and feel. They learned by playing.

Traditional teachers didn't understand this method. For them, the most important thing was to *teach*. For us, the most important thing was to *learn*. We also wanted children to help each other and to learn from their own experiences.

◆ ◆ ◆

Soon people in other countries wanted to know about my teaching method. Montessori schools were opened in many countries. By 1913, there were more than 100 Montessori schools in the USA. Alexander Graham Bell, the <u>inventor</u> of the telephone, believed in my method and became the leader of the American Montessori Society.

In 1915, I was invited to the USA and spoke at Carnegie Hall, a famous concert hall in New York. In San Francisco, I gave a course for teachers. We made a classroom with 21 students and a glass wall. Thousands of people came to watch our classes.

◆ ◆ ◆

In Europe, the First World War was destroying many lives. I decided to move to Barcelona in Spain where things were more <u>peaceful</u> than in Italy. I lived there for many years and travelled to many other countries to teach people about my method. In 1929, an international organization was started, the International Montessori Association. The organization encouraged parents and teachers to use the Montessori method.

In 1936, the Spanish <u>Civil War</u> started and I decided to move to Amsterdam, in the Netherlands. There were more than 200 Montessori schools in the Netherlands at that time. I continued to create new educational materials and give talks. I wanted people to use education for <u>peace</u>.

In 1939, I was invited to India to give talks and <u>train</u> teachers. The Second World War started that year and in 1940 the German army attacked the Netherlands. I couldn't go home to Amsterdam, so I stayed in India for several years and created courses for Indian teachers.

◆ ◆ ◆

For the rest of my life, I continued to train teachers and improve my method. I was given many <u>honours</u> for my work, such as the French Legion of Honour. I was also <u>nominated</u> three times for the Nobel Peace Prize because I believed in education for peace. I believed that education could improve people's lives. When I looked back at my long life, I was happy that my Montessori schools were able to do this.

The Life of Maria Montessori

1870   Maria Montessori was born in Chiaravalle, Italy.

1876   She started primary school in Rome.

1883   Maria started secondary school.

1886   She went to a technical college and did well in maths and science.

1890–1892   She studied science at the University of Rome and got her first degree in 1892.

1893   She was accepted by the medical school of the University of Rome.

1896   She became the first woman in Italy to become a doctor.

1896–1901   Maria studied children with mental problems in Rome University Hospital. In 1898, she became a director of a school in Rome for children with serious mental problems.

1906   Maria was asked by the government to work in a school for young children from poor families. In 1907, the first *Casa dei Bambini* (Children's House) was opened. Maria started to train teachers in her method.

1909–1915   Montessori schools opened around the world. Maria wrote many books during this time, such as *The Montessori Method* (1909).

1915   She was invited to give talks and train teachers in the USA.

1915–1936   Maria lived in Barcelona, Spain. She trained teachers and gave many talks about the Montessori Method. In 1929 the International Montessori Association was started.

1936   When the Spanish Civil War started, she moved to Amsterdam in the Netherlands.

1939   She went to India to give talks and train teachers.

1940   The Germans attacked the Netherlands in the Second World War. Maria had to stay in India until the war ended.

1946   She returned to the Netherlands and continued her work.

1947–1949   She wrote many more new books, such as *Peace and Education* (1949).

1949–1951   She continued to train teachers and improve her method. She won many honours, such as the French Legion of Honour.

1952   She died when she was 81 years old in the Netherlands.

Helen Keller

◆ ◆ ◆

1880–1968

the deaf and blind woman who
became a famous teacher

I became <u>blind</u> and <u>deaf</u> before I learned to speak. With the help of several special people, I learned to communicate. I used my communication skills to teach people about <u>blindness</u>. I also <u>fought for</u> the <u>rights</u> of women and workers.

◆ ◆ ◆

I was born in 1880, in Alabama, in the USA. When I was 19 months old, I became very sick with meningitis, a <u>disease</u> of the brain. I got better after the illness, but unfortunately I couldn't see or hear any more. I found it very difficult to learn and I became very angry. I was able to think, but I could not communicate my thoughts. It was a very difficult time for me and for my parents.

My mother and father wanted to help me but they didn't know what to do. Fortunately, I began to communicate with Martha Washington, who was 6 years old and the daughter of our cook. We created our own sign language when we played together. I enjoyed learning from Martha, but my mother realized that I needed professional help.

In 1886, my mother learned about the work of Alexander Graham Bell, the inventor of the telephone. He was working on the problems of the deaf. Maybe he could help? Bell told my mother about Perkins School for blind people and the school sent a special teacher to our home. Her name was Anne Sullivan.

◆ ◆ ◆

At first, I was a very difficult student, but Anne Sullivan was very kind to me. One day, we were getting water from the well when Anne drew some signs on my hand. I realized that she was writing the word 'water'. I was so excited! Within a few hours, I could 'read' more than 30 different words. At last, I could communicate with other people and they could communicate with me. Anne helped me to escape from my lonely world.

◆ ◆ ◆

When I was 8 years old, I went with Anne to the Perkins School for blind people. At the school, I was excited to discover that there were other children like me. We all learned from our teachers and from each other. I learned to read Braille in English and later in several other languages.

In 1894, Anne took me to New York and I studied at several different schools for the blind and deaf. I tried to learn to speak but it was difficult. My voice worked, but I didn't know how to use it properly. Only Anne and a few other people could understand me when I spoke.

◆ ◆ ◆

I studied hard and, in 1900, I started at university. Anne went with me to every class. She wrote the teachers' words on my hand. In 1904, I became the first deaf and blind person to get a degree. I was so happy and proud. And I knew that I wanted to use my communication skills to help other people.

At first, I worked with organizations that fought for women's rights. Then, in 1912, I started to work with workers' organizations. I discovered that some types of work made people blind. I wanted people to know about this problem, so I wrote a book in Braille about it.

In 1915, I started my own organization, Helen Keller International, which still teaches people about blindness. I wanted everyone to know that in many cases, blindness can be <u>prevented</u>.

◆ ◆ ◆

For many years, I travelled around the world and talked to groups of people about blindness. I communicated with Anne. She then spoke my words for me. Our talks became very popular and sometimes we earned up to

$2,000 a week. We gave the money to organizations that helped blind people.

When Anne became ill, Polly Thomson became my guide. Unfortunately, in 1936, Anne died. She did so much for me and I never forgot her.

◆ ◆ ◆

With the help of several special people, I wrote 12 books about my beliefs. I became famous because of the talks and the books. Important people wanted to meet me. I even met the King of England and the President of the USA.

Polly Thomson helped me with my work until she became very ill in 1957. After that, Winnie Corbally became my guide and travelled with me to teach people about blindness. Our work was helped by a theatre play, *The Miracle Worker* about the life of Anne Sullivan. In 1962, it became a popular film.

In 1964, I won an important award from the President of the USA for my work. The year after that, my name was added to the list of the most successful women in the USA – the Women's Hall of Fame. The names of my guides – Anne, Polly and Winnie – should be in that list too. In 1968, at the end of my life, I remembered Anne, Polly and Winnie. I felt proud of our work, which helped blind people around the world.

The Life of Helen Keller

1880   Helen Adams Keller was born in
        Tuscumbia, Alabama, USA.

1881   Helen became ill with meningitis (a disease
        of the brain) when she was 19 months old.
        She became deaf and blind because of the
        disease.

1882   She started playing with Martha
        Washington, a 6-year old girl. They created
        over 60 signs to communicate with each
        other.

1886   Helen's mother asked Alexander Graham
        Bell, the inventor of the telephone, for
        help. He told her about the Perkins School
        for blind children. The school sent Anne
        Sullivan to teach Helen. Anne taught Helen
        to communicate with other people. Anne
        stayed with Helen and helped her for
        49 years.

1888   Helen went to the Perkins School for blind
        children in Watertown, Massachusetts.
        Anne helped her to read and write in
        Braille.

1894   Helen moved to New York where she
        studied at several different schools for the
        blind and deaf.

1900   Helen started university at Radcliffe
        College in Cambridge, Massachusetts.

1904   She became the first deaf and blind person
        to get a degree.

1915   She started Helen Keller International,
        an organization to teach people about
        blindness.

1924   She started to travel around the world and
        give talks about blindness.

1936   Anne Sullivan died. Polly Thomson
        became her new guide. They travelled
        around the world and talked to groups
        about blindness.

1960   Polly Thomson died and Winnie Corbally
        became her guide.

1962   *The Miracle Worker*, a play about the life of
        Anne Sullivan, became a popular film.

1964   Helen received an award for her work from
        the President of the USA.

1965   Her name was added to the list of the
        most successful women in the USA – the
        Women's Hall of Fame.

1968   Helen Keller died at her home in Easton,
        Connecticut, USA. She was 88 years old.

Eva Perón

◆ ◆ ◆

1919–1952

the actress who helped poor and
sick people in Argentina

I was a famous actress in Argentina. I helped my husband, Juan Perón, to become President. I used my <u>power</u> to help sick and poor people. I also helped women to get the <u>vote</u> for the first time in Argentina.

◆ ◆ ◆

I was born in 1919 in Los Toldos in the Argentinian countryside. My mother was a poor country girl, but my father was a rich man from the city. Unfortunately, my father died when I was very young and life was very hard for my family. My mother worked hard to earn money. She made clothes for other people.

Four years after my father died, in 1930, we moved to a small apartment in the city of Junin. Life was very

Eva Perón's Argentina

difficult at first, but my brothers and sisters were growing up. Soon they got jobs. With their money, we moved to a larger home and I was able to start school.

I enjoyed school very much, but my favourite lessons were singing and acting. In 1933, I won a <u>role</u> in the school play – I was so excited! From that day, I knew that I wanted to be an actress. It was my dream.

In 1935, when I was 15 years old, my mother found me a place to live in Buenos Aires. It was exciting for me to be in this amazing city, but it was a time of great <u>economic</u> problems. Many people didn't have work and everywhere I went, I saw poor and hungry people in the streets.

Luckily I found a job so I had enough money to pay my rent. During the day I worked and, in the evenings, I joined a theatre group. Soon I was given my first role at the Comedias Theatre and, in 1936, I travelled with the theatre company around Argentina. I also got my first part in a film. I was only 17 years old and I was already an actress!

◆ ◆ ◆

In 1937, I started working for Radio El Mundo on a popular radio show. Radio El Mundo was the biggest radio company in Argentina and soon my name was well known. Then Radio Belgrano asked me to work for them on their show, *Great Women of History*. On the show, I played some famous roles – Queen Elizabeth the First of England was one of them.

I was no longer a poor girl from the countryside. Important people wanted to meet me and, by 1942, I had my own apartment in one of the best parts of the city. But then something happened that changed my life forever.

In January 1944, an <u>earthquake</u> hit the town of San Juan. It was terrible because 10,000 people were killed and many more were hurt. Juan Perón was an important political leader. He organized a concert to help the people of San Juan and I was invited to be in it.

After the concert, I talked to Juan Perón and learned about his political ideas. From that day, I had a new dream – I wanted Juan Perón to become the President of Argentina.

◆ ◆ ◆

On the radio, I talked every day about Juan's work and his ideas. Unfortunately, Juan had <u>powerful</u> <u>enemies</u> and they found him and put him in prison. On my radio show, I asked the people for help and, on 15th October 1945, 300,000 people came to the Casa Rosada (the President's house) in Buenos Aires. I stood on a <u>balcony</u> of the house and spoke to the people from my heart. Soon everyone was shouting, '<u>Free</u> Juan Perón! Free Juan Perón!'

Two days later, Juan was <u>free</u>. And the following day, Juan and I got married – we were so happy! We travelled together around Argentina and we both spoke at political meetings. I told the people that Juan could help them and their families. I also asked them to call me Evita (little Eva). We were a great success and, in 1946, Juan Perón became the President of Argentina.

◆ ◆ ◆

Suddenly, at the age of 27, I was the President's wife and the 'First Lady' of Argentina. I wanted to work hard and help the people. In 1947, Evita City was built to give homes to poor families. And, in 1948, I started the Eva Perón Foundation, an organization to help poor and sick people.

By 1950, the Foundation had received over $200 million and had 14,000 workers. We also gave out thousands of shoes and cooking materials and built hospitals and schools. I worked day and night and met with thousands of sick and poor people. I wanted to give them hope.

I also wanted women to have more political power. When Juan became President, women weren't able to <u>vote</u>. Juan and I fought to change this and I also started a new political party for women. It was called the Female Peronist Party. By 1951, the party had more than 500,000 women members. With the help of these women, Juan Perón became President for the second time.

◆ ◆ ◆

Many people wanted me to have a bigger political <u>role</u>, but I had to say no. I was already working too hard, sometimes more than 20 hours a day. And the problems I saw every day were making me ill. My husband asked me to take more rest, but the poor and sick people needed my help. I couldn't stop.

I was taken to hospital several times and lost a lot of weight. I was also in a lot of pain and the pain got worse and worse. I wanted to help my husband, but it wasn't possible. I wanted to see our country become a better place, but unfortunately this didn't happen. I was only 33 years old when I died, but people around the world still remember me. And many people in Argentina still think of me as their Evita.

The Life of Eva Perón

1919   Eva María Duarte was born in Los Toldos, Argentina.

1926   Her father, Juan Duarte, died in a car accident.

1930   Eva moved with her family to Junin, Argentina.

1933   She was given her first role in a school play and decided to become an actress.

1935   She moved to Buenos Aires and won a role with the Comedias Theatre company.

1936   She travelled around Argentina with the Comedias Theatre company. She also got a part in her first film.

1937   Eva began working as a radio actress with Radio El Mundo. Later that year she started working for Radio Belgrano on their show, *Great Women of History.*

1942   She bought her own apartment in Recoleta, one of the richest areas of Buenos Aires.

1944   10,000 people were killed in an earthquake in San Juan. Eva was invited to be in a concert to help the people of San Juan. After the concert, she met Juan Perón for the first time.

1945   Eva talked about Juan Perón's political ideas on her radio show. On 9th October, Juan's enemies put him in prison. Eva spoke to 300,000 people from the balcony of the Casa Rosada. Two days later Juan was free. A day later, Juan and Eva were married.

1946   Juan became the President of Argentina.

1947   Evita City was built to give homes to poor families. Women won the right to vote for the first time in Argentina.

1948   Eva started the Eva Perón Foundation, an organization to help poor people.

1951   Juan Perón became President of Argentina for the second time. The Female Peronist Party had more than 500,000 members by this time. They helped Juan to become President again.

1952   Eva Perón became very sick and died. She was 33 years old.

Nancy Wake

◆ ◆ ◆

1912–2011

the woman who became a spy in the
Second World War

ol 25

I fought with the French <u>Resistance</u> against the Germans in the Second World War. I got <u>weapons</u> for the Resistance <u>fighters</u> and helped fighters to escape. I was part of the final <u>victory</u> against the Germans in 1945.

◆ ◆ ◆

I was born in New Zealand, but I grew up in Sydney, Australia. When I was 16 years old, I left home and got a job as a nurse in the Australian countryside. In 1932, I received a surprise – £200 from my aunt. It was a lot of money at that time and I decided to spend it. I went to Sydney Harbour and bought a ticket to North America.

I enjoyed the journey on the ship and then travelled around the USA and Canada. When I wasn't travelling, I

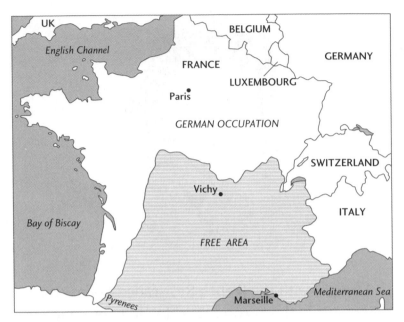

France after June 1940

worked as a waitress to earn some money. After a while, I moved to Britain. I wanted to work on a newspaper, so I studied to become a newspaper reporter.

I got my first job on a newspaper in Paris, where I learned to speak French. I went to Germany and Austria for the newspaper. I saw the terrible things that Adolf Hitler and his <u>Nazi</u> party were doing in their country. I realized then that the Nazis were very dangerous. And they wanted to rule the whole of Europe.

◆ ◆ ◆

In 1940, the Germans attacked France and <u>occupied</u> most of the country. I was already living in the south of

France, where I married my first husband, a businessman, Henri Fiocca. We both hated the Nazis and wanted to help in the war against them.

I began to work for the French Resistance in Marseille. I delivered secret messages to the Resistance fighters and I also helped fighters to escape. The Germans tried to catch me. I used <u>false papers</u> and changed my appearance so they didn't recognize me. In 1943, the Germans caught me, but luckily I escaped.

It was too dangerous for me to stay in France. I had to leave my husband and go over the Pyrenees mountains to Spain. From Spain, I escaped to London and joined the British army. I was a little surprised when the British wanted me to become a <u>spy</u>. They wanted me to be part of a secret army, which helped the French Resistance.

The training with the British army was very hard and I worked night and day to learn the special skills. I learned how to look after <u>injured</u> fighters. I also learned to kill. And so I became a spy and set off on my first <u>mission</u> to France.

◆ ◆ ◆

I arrived in France on 29th April 1944. At first, the French Resistance didn't believe that I could help them. They didn't think that a woman could be a fighter. A Resistance leader told one of his men, 'This woman could be an <u>enemy</u>. Ask her to go for a walk with you. When no one is around, kill her!' They didn't realize I could speak French. I understood everything.

When we went for the walk, I told the man, 'If you attack me, I will kill you first.' He believed me and took me back to the camp. At last, the Resistance allowed me to join them. I got weapons from Britain and also took part in their attacks against the Germans. We blew up railway lines and stole German weapons. On one occasion, I killed a German soldier. On another, I killed a Resistance fighter who was working for the Germans.

♦ ◆ ♦

Our attacks against the Germans were very <u>successful</u>, but it was difficult to keep everything secret. Many local people were frightened of the German soldiers and sometimes they gave the Germans information about our plans. On one occasion, someone told the Germans about our secret <u>radio transmitter</u>. Our radio operator destroyed our <u>codes</u> so the Germans didn't discover our secrets.

I cycled 500 kilometres to get new codes. When German soldiers stopped me, I told them, 'I'm going to visit my aunt who's very ill.' After three days, I got the codes. Everyone said that I was very brave, but I didn't think about that. I had to do it. It was part of my job.

With the new codes, I could send secret messages to Britain. We could receive new weapons and start our attacks again. Our attacks were important. They stopped the <u>progress</u> of around 50,000 German soldiers. These soldiers weren't able to fight the British army, which was arriving in the north of France.

◆ ◆ ◆

In September 1944, I received orders to go to Paris. In Paris, I helped the British and French armies in the final months of the war. On 8th May 1945, we heard the wonderful news. The war was over and the victory was ours!

I wanted to return home to my husband. I was shocked to discover that he was dead. He was killed by the Germans in 1943. It was time for me to start a new life.

I went back to Australia and tried to become a politician. I wasn't successful and life seemed boring after the war. I then moved to the UK for several years and I got an office job with the British <u>secret service</u>.

I was happy to receive many <u>honours</u> for my work in the war, such as the George Medal from the British. And at the end of my life, I felt proud to be part of one of the most important victories in history. The victory brought <u>peace</u> and <u>freedom</u> to Europe.

The Life of Nancy Wake

1912   Nancy Wake was born in Wellington, New Zealand.

1914   Nancy and her family moved to Sydney, Australia.

1928   She left home and worked as a nurse in the Australian countryside.

1932–1936   She received £200 from her aunt. Nancy used the money to travel around North America. She then moved to London, where she studied to become a newspaper reporter. She got her first job on a newspaper in Paris. She visited Germany and Austria and met Adolf Hitler in 1933.

1939   The Second World War started. On 1st September, Germany attacked Poland. Two days later, Britain and France began to fight against the Germans.

1940   Nancy joined the French Resistance in Marseille. She delivered secret messages and helped Resistance fighters to escape from the Germans.

1943   Nancy was caught by the Germans, but she escaped to Britain. She joined the British army and trained to be a spy.

1944   On 29th April, Nancy arrived in occupied
        France and worked with the French
        Resistance. On 11th September, she was
        sent to Paris to help the British and French
        armies.

1945   The Second World War ended. Nancy
        received many honours after the war, such
        as the George Medal from the UK.

1949   Nancy returned to Australia. She tried to
        become a politician in Sydney, but wasn't
        successful.

1951–1958   She moved back to England and got an
        office job with the British secret service. In
        1957, she married a British army pilot, John
        Forward.

1960   She returned to Australia with her husband.

1988   She won Officer of the Legion of Honour,
        one of the highest honours from the French
        government.

1997   Her husband died after 40 years of
        marriage.

2001   Nancy moved to London and lived at the
        Stafford Hotel.

2011   Nancy died in London, England. She was
        98 years old.

accept VERB
to allow someone to join a
school, club or other
organization

action UNCOUNTABLE NOUN
something that you do for
political reasons, because you
want to change a situation
NOUN
a movement that you make with
your body when you are doing
something such as kicking a ball

activist NOUN
a person who tries to make
changes in society

arrest VERB
to take someone to a police
station, because they may have
broken the law

award NOUN
a prize that a person is given for
doing something well

balcony NOUN
a place where you can stand or
sit on the outside of a building,
above the ground

belief NOUN
a strong feeling that you have

when you know that something
must be true

blind ADJECTIVE
not able to see

blindness UNCOUNTABLE NOUN
the state of not being able to
see anything

Braille UNCOUNTABLE NOUN
a system of printing for blind
people. The letters are printed
as groups of raised dots that you
can feel with your fingers

campaign VERB
to do a number of actions over a
period of time in order to get a
particular result
NOUN
a number of things that a group
of people do over a period of
time in order to get a particular
result

celebrate VERB
to do something enjoyable for a
special reason

civil war NOUN
a war between different groups
of people who live in the same
country

code NOUN
a secret way to replace the words
in a message with other words or
symbols, so that some people will
not understand the message

create VERB
to make something happen or
exist for the first time

deaf ADJECTIVE
not able to hear

disease NOUN
an illness that affects people,
animals or plants

earthquake NOUN
a sudden strong movement of the
Earth's surface that can do a lot
of damage to buildings and roads

economic ADJECTIVE
connected with the organization
of the money and industry of a
country

educational ADJECTIVE
done or made in order to teach
someone something

enemy NOUN
a person or army who is fighting
against you in a war

equal ADJECTIVE
used for saying that different
groups of people should be
treated in the same way

equality UNCOUNTABLE NOUN
the fair treatment of all the
people in a group

false papers NOUN
documents that are supposed to
prove who someone is, but which
are not official because they
were made illegally

fight
to fight for something PHRASE
to try very hard to get something

fighter NOUN
a person who takes part in a war

find
to find your way PHRASE
to get somewhere by choosing
the right way to go

free VERB
to help someone to get out of a
place where they are a prisoner or
being controlled by other people

ADJECTIVE
used for describing someone
who is not a prisoner, or who is
not controlled by other people
any more

freedom UNCOUNTABLE NOUN
the state of not being controlled
by other people

guide NOUN
someone whose job is to help a
blind person move around

honour NOUN
a special award that is given
to someone

illegal ADJECTIVE
not allowed by law

injured ADJECTIVE
having a damaged body after
being in a fight or battle

injury NOUN
damage to a person's or an
animal's body

inventor NOUN
a person who has invented
something, or whose job is to
invent things

judge NOUN
a person whose job is to decide
how criminals should be
punished

law NOUN
a rule that everyone in a country
has to obey

lawyer NOUN
a person whose job is to give
people advice about the law and
to help them when they are in a
court of law

marriage NOUN
the period of time during which
two people are married

medical ADJECTIVE
relating to the study of illness
and injuries and how to treat or
prevent them

mental ADJECTIVE
relating to the mind

mission NOUN
an important job that someone
has to do, especially one that
involves travelling to a different
country

Nazi NOUN
a member of the political party
led by Adolf Hitler, which held
power in Germany from 1933
to 1945

ADJECTIVE
relating to the Nazis

nominate VERB
to formally suggest that
someone should get a job or
be given a prize

nursemaid NOUN
a woman or girl who is paid to
look after young children

occupy VERB
to move into a country or city
and use force to control it

owner NOUN
someone who owns a slave

peace UNCOUNTABLE NOUN
a situation where there is not
a war

peaceful ADJECTIVE
not involving war or violence

power NOUN
someone's ability to make other
people do what they want
them to

powerful ADJECTIVE
able to control people and events

prevent VERB
to make sure that something bad
does not happen

professional ADJECTIVE
relating to the work that is done
by someone who has had special
training

progress UNCOUNTABLE NOUN
movement in a forward direction
1 to travel a long distance
towards where you want to go in
a journey
2 to start to be successful in the
course of a process that you are
trying to develop

protest VERB
to say or show publicly that you
do not approve of something

NOUN
an event where a lot of people
come together in public to say
that they do not approve of a
situation

punish VERB
to make someone suffer in some
way because they have done
something wrong

radio transmitter NOUN
a piece of equipment that you
use to send messages by radio

resistance NOUN
a group of people who are
fighting against an army that has
taken control of their country

revolution NOUN
when a group of people changes
their country's government by
using force

right NOUN
permission to do something that
you have because it is the law

role NOUN
1 the character that an actor
plays in a film or a play
2 the particular position
someone has in society or in a
company

route NOUN
a way from one place to another

secret service NOUN
a government department whose job is to find out enemy secrets and to stop the enemy from finding out its own government's secrets

slavery UNCOUNTABLE NOUN
the system by which people are owned by other people as slaves

spy NOUN
a person whose job is to find out secret information about another country or organization

successful ADJECTIVE
doing or getting the results you wanted

technical ADJECTIVE
involving machines, processes and materials that are used in science and industry

train VERB
1 to teach people the skills that they need in order to do something
2 to learn the skills that you need in order to be able to do something

victory NOUN
a success in a war or a competition

vote VERB
to take part in an election by saying which politician you want to be the winner
NOUN
the right to say which politician you want to be the winner of an election

weapon NOUN
an object such as a gun, that is used for killing or hurting people

well NOUN
a deep hole in the ground from which people take water or oil

Collins
English Readers

AMAZING PEOPLE READERS AT OTHER LEVELS:

Level 2

Amazing Aviators
978-0-00-754495-0

Amazing Architects and Artists
978-0-00-754496-7

Amazing Composers
978-0-00-754502-5

Amazing Mathematicians
978-0-00-754503-2

Amazing Medical People
978-0-00-754509-4

Level 3

Amazing Explorers
978-0-00-754497-4

Amazing Writers
978-0-00-754498-1

Amazing Philanthropists
978-0-00-754504-9

Amazing Performers
978-0-00-754505-6

Amazing Scientists
978-0-00-754510-0

Level 4

Amazing Thinkers and Humanitarians
978-0-00-754499-8

Amazing Scientists
978-0-00-754500-1

Amazing Writers
978-0-00-754506-3

Amazing Leaders
978-0-00-754507-0

Amazing Entrepreneurs and Business People
978-0-00-754511-7

Visit **www.collinselt.com/readers** for language activities, teacher's notes, and to find out more about the series.

Collins
English Readers

Also available at this level

Level 1
CEF A2

Amazing Inventors
978-0-00-754494-3

Amazing Entrepreneurs and Business People
978-0-00-754501-8

Amazing Leaders
978-0-00-754492-9

Amazing Performers
978-0-00-754508-7

Sign up for our emails at **www.collinselt.com**
to receive free teaching and/or learning resources, as well as the most
up-to-date news about new publications, events, and competitions.

POWERED BY COBUILD

www.collinselt.com   /collinselt   @CollinsELT